The Last Words of Isparhecher

Creek Indian Chief

The Last Words of Isparhecher

Creek Indian Chief

Ora V. Eddleman

1903

Eddleman, Ora V.

The Last Words of Isparhecher: Creek Indian Chief/Ora V. Edleman

p. cm.

1. Isparhecher, Creek Chief (1829-1902). 2. Creek Indians--Biography. I. Title.

E 99 .C9
973.0497

ISBN-10   1986426350

ISBN-13   978-1983426353

Cover Photo - Isparhecher, Chief of the Creek Nation, 1895-1899

Table of Contents

When, on December 24th, 1902, ex-Chief Isparhecher lay dying, he called to his bedside a young full-blood Creek Indian man, Turner Taylor, who has spent much of his life with the old Chief, acting as his interpreter and in many ways helping him. Below are the words which Isparhecher spoke to Turner Taylor, asking that they be 'written and published among his people.' Turner Taylor wrote them in Creek just as the old Chief uttered them, and, after Isparhecher's death he forwarded the letter to Chief Pleasant Porter, who translated it for the

Editor of *Twin Territories Indian Magazine*, and it is here published for the first time.

Ora V. Eddleman

"I have returned to my home conscious that I am dangerously sick. I am aware that I will be with you but a little while. This I wish you to know, You have been my friend and, as you speak the white man's tongue, at any time I wished, to talk to a white man you have truly interpreted, my words. In our lives we have been united and as death is to part us give me your hand in a last farewell. I charge you now with haste to put my last words on paper. I am stricken with disease and, I am not to withstand it. It will soon overwhelm me. It has been ordained that disease was to conquer me.

I have always maintained that I was a true man and in the conflict of arms, mid shot and. shell, I have demeaned myself as a man and passed. through wars unharmed.

"In this manner, day and time, it is the will of Him who reigns on high that I am to fulfill and hand back the life he gave me. Before passing I feel that I should say that none will ever rise up in my Nation and, people in my likeness and character. I have held in my Nation the most important trusts that could, be placed in the keeping of any man -- even to that of Chief of the Nation. I have from time to time fulfilled the most important missions in arranging certain agreements with the United. States Government, all of which have been discharged with fidelity, and, to the interest of my people. Latest, I was selected to attend to the final settlement of the Loyal Creek Claim. I am stopped by the relentless hand of death. It was to be so. The Loyal Creeks must now think for themselves and act for the best.

"My people and nation are now held, firmly in the power of the American nation. Those of you who survive, I charge you to conduct yourself with discretion and honorably. There have been thoughts of leaving our home and country and seeking a resting place elsewhere. Those who so contemplate should think carefully before continuing in their plans. I know not the hour of my departure. It will not be long, so I wish you to know it. There can be no charge of fault made against anyone for the present trying conditions with which we are surrounded. Those who are now near me and around me, and who will survive me, must remember my charge to think well and act with discretion under all circumstances.

"I have somewhat more to say: My grave and last resting place shall be after this fashion, so made that my head shall lie toward the rising sun. This was the custom of the forefathers and invariably followed by them. When a person has been prostrated by sickness the teachers of Christianity are often called in and, prayer and songs are made for them. That must not be done in my case. I forbid it. Death will come to me when He who is on high wills it so to be. That is all I have to say. I am now ready to die."

Thus ended the life of the "Grand old man of the Creeks," as Isparhecher was sometimes called. He led an eventful life, and passed through many important times among Creek people. Admired by many, criticized by many, yet none could say that he did not stick to his principles and live up to his own belief in all matters.

The life history of Isparhecher is an interesting one. In 1836 a party of Creek Indians moved from the old Nation in

Alabama to Indian Territory, among whom were the parents of Isparhecher, his father Yarteca Tustennugee, and his mother, Kechahteh. Isparhecher was then about eight years of age, so the greater part of his youth was spent on the banks of the Canadian, in Indian Territory.

His opportunities were few. The surroundings of the Indian boy in those days were not as they are today, so the Indian lad grew up as best he might; the loss of his parents necessitated his being early thrown upon his own resources, and so the eventful career of Isparhecher began.

Much can be written of the life of this man both praiseworthy and otherwise, as is the case regarding any man. He was ambitious and persistent, and patriotic, as he understood patriotism, to his own people. At the outbreak of the Civil War, Isparhecher, and other young Creek Indians, were organized into a company under command of Col. McIntosh in the Confederate army. Not wishing to leave Indian Territory when the Confederates were ordered to do so, Isparhecher remained here, and afterwards joined the Union army, being mustered out of service at Ft. Gibson in 1865. Afterwards, Isparhecher held several positions in his Nation, then occurred what was known as the Isparhecher, or Green Peach War. The trouble arose over Isparhecher's determination to drive from the country the thieves and outlaws who had for years infested it. This determination led to several skirmishes between the outlaws and Isparhecher's lighthorsemen, and on one occasion one man was killed by the officers. At another time, the officers at a council, or party meeting, arrested a man who was discovered carrying a pistol, contrary to law. The prisoner was turned over to the officers of another district and placed in a building. This building was soon besieged by a mob of Isparhecher's enemies who, in the successful attempt to rescue the prisoner, killed one of the officers. All these complications reaching headquarters, no doubt greatly exaggerated, created ill reports against Isparhecher, and he was charged with creating sedition. He was told that the lighthorsemen were on their way to arrest him. Not being able to prove his innocence, Isparhecher was forced to either give up or fight for his protection. The latter he did with the aid of friends. After a fierce conflict with the Union force, with a victory for Isparhecher, the latter went over into the Cherokee Nation, where he remained until informed that he would not be disturbed if he returned home. But once more he was pursued by militia, and this time, Old Isparhecher went to the Sac and Fox reservation, from there to the Comanche country, where the Chief, Asa Habbe, offered him protection. The two became good friends, and Isparhecher and his followers remained with Asa Habbe until spring, when Isparhecher was again told that he might return unmolested to his own country. This time a reconciliation was affected, and, so closed the Isparhecher, or Green Peach War.

But Isparhecher was not an old man yet -- at least not inactive. That same year he was nominated. principal Chief but was defeated; once more he experienced defeat for the same office, but a third time proved the rule, and he was elected Chief of the Creek Nation in September, 1895, entering upon the duties of his office the fifth day of the following December.

To enter into the details of Isparhecher's chieftaincy would require much space, for the Creek Nation passed through many trying ordeals while the old man reigned. Many important events transpired, treaties were made, one with the Dawes Commission on September 27, 1897, which failed of ratification on the following November by a majority vote of the Nation. The Curtis Act of June 28, 1898, now became effective, and the Creek Courts were abolished, together with the office of Judge, Prosecuting Attorney, and Lighthorsemen. Another Agreement was made on February 1, 1899, which was ratified by popular vote of the Creek people, but not by Congress.

After four years of Isparhecher's rule, Chief Porter assumed the duties of Chief on December 5, 1899, and the career of the Creek people grows brighter as time goes on.

These, then, are some of the principal events in Creek history that occurred during the life of Isparhecher. There was some of romance in the life of the old

Chief, also. He was four times married; to Pollkissut, a daughter of Poskofa; again, at her death, to Wahnahka Barnett, and after her death to Latissa, a Creek woman. Then, while in Washington, he met and married his laundress, a white woman, who returned to Indian Territory with him, but soon after returned to her home in Washington.

But the old man is gone. The Creeks, his people for whom he desired so much, are entering upon a new condition of affairs, and soon the old days will have passed into oblivion. But the words of the old Chief, who could neither read nor write, and who notwithstanding all the ordeals through which he passed as best he could -- his admonition to his people "to act for the best -- to conduct themselves with discretion, and honorably under all circumstances," make a fitting farewell from the lips of a man who devoted his life as best he knew how, to his people and to his country. The old Chief -- by some considered, wily, shrewd and ignorant of the best course to pursue, by many followers loved, by his enemies hated, by some feared -- whatever virtues or whatever misdeeds may be laid at his door, Isparhecher will not soon be forgotten.

Chickasha Weekly Express

Chickasha, Indian Territory

January 2, 1903

Vol. 11, No. 22

Horace W. Shepard, Editor

Obituary on Isparhecher

Former Chief isparhecher of the Creek Indians died suddenly at Okmulgee, at the age of 90 years. He had been prominent in Creek Affairs for three score years and had connected with every treaty of importance between the United States government and Indians during that time. Recently he was chosen to represent the tribe in Washington on matters of importance concerning the Creeks.

Made in the USA
Middletown, DE
07 June 2022

66797380R00018